The stories in this book reflect the author's recollection of events. Some names, locations, and identifying characteristics have been changed to protect the privacy of those depicted. Dialogue has been recr   om memory.

Crayons and The Purgatory Journal

A Childhood Memoir

By: Gina Y. Talone

Table of Contents

Section 1

- Preface
- Introduction: My Reflection
- Prelude: Spirit of Advocacy
- Chapter One: My Immigrant Ancestry

Section 2

- Chapter Two: My Family and My Home
- Chapter Three: Prayer at Home
- Chapter Four: Parochial School
- Chapter Five: Confession
- Chapter Six: First Holy Communion
- Chapter Seven: Lent & Easter
- Chapter Eight: Guardian Angel
- Chapter Nine: Physical manifestations
- Chapter Ten: Sexuality
- Chapter Eleven: Purgatory and Indulgences

Section 3

- Chapter Twelve: When I Told Mom
- Chapter Thirteen: Recovery

Section 4

- Conclusion
- Spirituality Calvary Cemetery
- Changes with Vatican II

Dedicated to:

My dear sister Mary

Two years before Mary's death, I shared my writings with my beloved sister. We had much discussion. With her passing away, in December of 2017, I now have the courage to publish my experiences. A big shout-out to her in heaven!

SECTION 1

Preface:

Place in History: In the 1950's the disorder now named "OCD Scrupulosity" was unknown to most, no meds or treatment readily available.

The Disorder: The Scrupulosity feature of OCD *has now been identified*; it focuses on doubt, guilt, sin, repetitive prayer and fear for salvation.

The Person: I was a child at the time. As a published writer, I have the skills to articulate the experiences. This was reality for me, I endured it, recovered from it and later in life decided to uncover it! *I am speaking as a layperson reliving memories.*

Religion, Tradition and Environment: As I understand, any form of religion, doctrine or theology can provide a foundation for which scrupulosity can attach, but religion is not the cause. Neither is tradition or environment. I was born with a disorder; it is a part of me. We cannot change history but I will show you how *the culture in the 1950s flamed the fire of my disorder.*

Introduction: My reflection

I begin my memoir as an adult. Let's go back in time:

Do you remember the period that was the 1950's? Remember when mental illness had a harrowing stigma? People would say in a hushed whisper, "There must be something wrong with him or her." Adding to the misfortune, much of the treatment back then was primitive. Perhaps better said, treatment was at the doorstep to the larger structure of efficacy, currently in place, for easing the symptoms of mental suffering.

A perfect storm one might say was an extremely sensitive child, under the direction of parents with a severe religiosity, attending a parochial school where many a day existed of rules, guilt and fear of punishment. At the time, my immigrant ancestry felt both an anchor and a safety net within the confines and the direction of the Church's rules and regulations. This sense of loyalty to the Catholic Church was taught and passed down generationally. So, wasn't this a positive thing? What was wrong with that, you may ask, and how did others survive? Many others matured within this culture without any repercussions. Unfortunately, I was not one of them. With the extreme rules existing within my environment, it was all like fertilizer to a garden. Spontaneity and joy were missing from my life.

With the disorder, I can say the suffering was a tortuous event. I felt a sense of being alone and unaware of the existence of the illness, one which was pervasive and debilitating. Historically, my diagnosis was a probable "nervous breakdown," as my parents sought help from the primary doctor. As this occurred in the 1950's, neither psychiatric drugs nor behavior therapy were readily available. To the sufferer, ***especially a child***, the OCD symptoms were an intrusive invasion of the mind, but I was oblivious to the existence of an illness. My parents were unaware of which symptoms were associated with such an illness as OCD. However, they still held on the prevailing awareness of the stigma of 'mental illness.'

The following presentation is my own and based upon my symptoms. I will ask you as we progress: Do you think I experienced childhood Obsessive-Compulsive Disorder (OCD) with Scrupulosity? I truly believe this is the disorder under which I suffered. Regarding my writings, I must reiterate: I am not qualified to discuss the medical and psychological basis, nor the development of Obsessive-Compulsive Disorder with Scrupulosity. I don't pretend to be and it is not my intent. ***I can only describe the torment and suffering which I endured***, which closely follows the description of this disorder. I cannot separate the symptoms from the cause. You may be thinking: What is my motivation? It is very simple. To tell what occurred during those dark days and how I survived.

This memoir is not an autobiography and not in chronological order, except for excerpts of my ancestry. Rather, there are sections listed by subject, many of which are the Blessed Sacraments of the Church. These were my occurrences that fell within these practices, and my thoughts as a child. There is no intent to mimic or pass judgement. Could there be historical value in the sharing of my childhood psychological suffering? I hope you find it to be so. In either event, I write the following in a spirit of advocacy for any child suffering with a similar disorder such as OCD and Scrupulosity.

Prelude: Spirit of Advocacy

Do you think secrets can be buried? Can they be hushed into the pounding valves of our hearts? Maybe so. But they can't stay clandestine forever. Eventually they thread and weave from your heart into the darkness of your soul, only to soar at the most unexpected of times! You see, the secret of my childhood disorder was one of these. I no longer find the need to bury this private experience, but rather to utilize it in a productive way. I am now a senior lady with a desire to write and to inspire others. God had given me the disorder; I was born with it. I now own it.

Chapter One: My immigrant ancestry

Today I still love and cherish the memories of my parents and I still love my Catholic Church. I've received hope and healing from both. I would not be the person I am today, without their contributions to my development as a child. Both of my parents were people of high integrity. At that time in history, my church was steeped in its traditional archaic culture. I knew no other Church.

Mom was a caring and loving person who would reach out to others. She wasn't active with the school or community; she didn't drive a car for one thing and secondly, she had limits to her self-confidence. In contrast, Pop was authoritative and self-driven. He had few friends or hobbies and was consumed with his construction business. Although Mom had a limited education, she loved to read, especially about the life of Christ and the many Saints. She was wise in many ways, but she exhibited a lot of fears: fears of Pop and his sisters in the "old country," of the Pastor of the Church and all its rules. With these fears, I don't think she ever waivered.

I ask you, doesn't our ancestry lay the groundwork for a lot of things? Not only for the color of our hair and eyes, of how tall or short we are, but also for our social, religious and cultural attitudes? Mine was so integrally involved in my own childhood development, that I present it in detail. I love my ancestors for their courage, sacrifice and enduring qualities. They were heroes in a lot of ways. *However, with the evolution of this culture came extreme religiosity.*

Ancestry on my Mother's side:

My grandparents were born in a small town in northern Italy, near the Austrian border. It was a quaint town in a green covered valley surrounded by the towering Dolomite Alps, a place of breathtaking beauty. The people there were hardworking peasants who lived off the land, and their lives were simple and wholesome.

My maternal Grandma was born in 1880 and my Grandpa in 1872. They were good religious people. My Grandpa left for Austria when he was 11 years old to work in the brick foundries. He worked there for many years enduring many hardships. Men and boys all had to migrate to France, Switzerland, and Germany to find work. The women all stayed home and took care of the children and fields. The young girls went away also to work as maids.

My maternal grandparents were married in 1905 in the town church which was very beautiful. Grandma was 25 and my Grandpa was 33. Their first child died shortly after birth. Then a daughter was born, named Lena. Times in Italy were difficult, so they and their little family came to America to enable my grandpa to find steady work. My mother Rosa was born in 1910.

My Grandfather then became severely ill and had to be hospitalized. Due to this prolonged illness, my grandma and her daughters had to go back to Italy, until her husband recovered and could work again. They stayed in Italy for three years. In 1915, my Grandpa regained his health and called for them to return to America.

My mother Rosa remembered the boat in which they crossed the Atlantic. It took about 3 weeks on the ocean. She and Lena became very seasick. Upon their return, it was a hard adjustment for my grandmother to adjust to living in the poorest sections of the city, after coming from the beautiful country in the Alps. They moved from place to place many times, and had to attend many different schools.

The narrative below is taken from my mother Rosa's journals and is written in her voice. Many of the notes seem to echo the eventual thought patterns in the evolving family!

My Mom stayed home all the time, it seemed she never went anywhere. During her time at home, she loved to crochet and needlework. She never went to church because she did not have the clothes, but she always saw that we went on Sunday and Confession on Saturday. She always remembered what her parents taught her. To raise her children with "Temor

Di Dio" which means *"Fear of the Lord."* Mom told us at an early age that there was no Santa and we didn't expect anything. We always had friends to play with and my childhood was happy. Lena and I were always together and everyone called us Siamese Twins. We were inseparable.

We lived in the poor section of the city until 1922 when we moved to a small house many miles out into the County. The trees and fields of wild flowers and the creeks were so beautiful. I remember it was like a paradise.

The family was so happy in their little dream house. Just 4 small rooms, no closets, an outhouse. But it wasn't long before Mom transformed it. She planted many flowers, the boys built a windmill and a pond with goldfish and a bird house. They were very creative and talented and always kept busy. Mom kept the children pretty much under her wing. She was a strong woman and was well loved and respected.

We children went to school at the local Catholic school. I perceived myself as just average, but I loved to read. I would read anything I could. Mom always discouraged reading. She said the children would only learn bad things. The world always seemed ugly to Mom and she always tried to protect her children from it. She taught her daughters domestic chores like sewing and crocheting. Lena went to work at a lamp manufacturing company in the city. She helped the family a lot.

Then in February 1923 I quit school and went to work with Lena. But it wasn't easy. I had to go to the Board of Education many times before they would give me a permit for I lacked 5 months to being 14. Every time I went *on the streetcar, I would get sick and vomit on the street, but I was determined to get the permit. Then finally the lady felt sorry for me and gave me the permit.*

I was hired, but not before I went to the hospital for a chest x-ray for they thought I had tuberculosis. I weighed 87 lbs. I remember going on the streetcar all alone and how embarrassed I was when I had to expose my chest to the doctor. But I was given a good report. I was placed in the drapery department. I worked hard and give it all I had. I was making $75 every two weeks and that was good money in those days. Mom had it a little easier. We paid off the house and did some repair work like finishing the basement and installing a toilet.

Mario then came into my life. Mario came from Toledo and had worked in the ceramic tile industry; he was sent here to work at a hospital as a foreman. This was during the depression and jobs were hard to find. He later came to visit us and asked me for a date. I will never forget, I did not have a nice dress. So, mom made me a dress from a pair of organdy curtains, a light green. It turned out very pretty and it looked nice on me. I did have a nice figure at the time and was considered pretty. I was very shy and did not have all the social graces that some girls had.

This was the time of the roaring 20's with the Charleston and girls bobbing their hair and skirts were getting shorter and things were changing. Mario kept coming and most of the time he would just sit and talk to mom about our home town and his family. At first, mom did not care for him. Although she would tell me that he came from a good family for she knew them well. They were neighbors in Italy.

Mario had a way of insulting people. He would come right out and tell you what he thought. Mom was the same way, and that was why they clashed. He was very serious at first; I didn't think he was much fun. Mario was very handsome when he was young. Curly black hair just starting to get grey and blue eyes. He was 29 at the time; we had much in common and we got along well. I admired some of his qualities.

Moving forward, I lost my father in 1932. My brothers weren't earning much money; I had to keep working to support the family. Those were hard times, as there was no welfare at the time, so we had to make the best of it. Mom managed very well with the chickens and rabbits and pigeons. We always had good meals, but no dessert.

Then in 1935, Mario and I got married and I quit work. We bought a house in a local township; it was a beautiful home and it seemed like a palace to me. I soon became pregnant but miscarried at 4 months. I continued to visit Mom every day; it was hard for me to break away. I then gave birth to Mary in 1936 and to Louis in 1939.

When Louis was just 9 months old, Mario was bitten by a dog. The dog was not to be found. He went to our primary doctor. He would not give Mario shots, so he went to a specialist. Well, the specialist gave him a series of shots. The serum shocked his nervous system and another specialist was called in. He was hospitalized and was in a coma for 5 days. He was very fortunate to have survived for the specialist said that only 2 men have ever been recorded to survive the allergy. Mario made medical history. The specialist said that someone must have been praying for him and that he had a strong will to live and a strong constitution. He had a catheter in him for 6 weeks and it was a year before he recovered. It was a very difficult time for him, with the business to attend to, but he had strong willpower.

With the circle of life, my sister Lena became very sick and died at the age of 33 but another son, William, was born to us in 1942. Then my mother became ill and passed away from liver cancer in March of 1944. To me her death was devastating.

We then had a daughter we named Gina who was born in 1947. She was born at a maternity clinic across from Calvary Cemetery. Then a son we named Michael came along in 1952. We now had five children. At that point, we needed a bigger home, so Mario built a house in a new subdivision, further out in the county. We moved into the new home after Thanksgiving in 1952.

Rosa's notes about my father:

I feel I must write about my husband Mario's family. Mario was the 6th child of 10 children. His father was a merchant with a small store. He would travel with his goods to different towns with his horse and wagon. It was a very meager livelihood. His mother was a saintly woman who took care of the home and the fields. They kept cows for milk, cheese and butter. It was hard work. The house they lived in dated back to the 17th century. The girls all had to work as maids at an early age in France and Milan and Venice. They had a hard time raising their children, especially during the first World War.

Mario was just 14 when he had to leave home and go to work at the front with his father. The Germans occupied their town; they had to share their food with the Germans and the family was often hungry. Mario experienced many traumatic times at this early age, experiences which he never forgot.

After a few years, Mario and Tony saw future opportunity in America, so they immigrated to the United States. Mario was 18 years old and Tony 16, aboard a boat named the <u>Giuseppe Verdi.</u>

There is a brick on Ellis Island dedicated to my father. *Mario's destiny was to meet Rosa and to become my father.*

In reflection, many years later:

When Pop was in America he bragged that he was an Italian; when he returned to

Italy, he bragged about being an American! He had seen the best and the worst of both cultures. During this cultural period in America in the thirties and forties, Italians were still discriminated against, and there was rivalry between Catholic Irish and Catholic Italians. Both of my parents were victims of this discrimination. Pop fought to overcome the alleged unfair treatment and it was difficult for him to keep from holding a grudge. These feelings prevailed.

While Pop loved the American dream, Mom was secure in her home with her devotion to the Catholic religion. Pop had high aspirations for us children, probably due to his background of poverty in Italy as a young boy. It was something which he never forgot.

As children, our motivation was not so much about personal development, as it was trying to please Pop and receive affirmation from him. Mom seemed to love and admire us as we were. However, Mom had developed an allegiance to the church that was first and foremost in her life.

SECTION 2

Chapter Two: My family and my home

It is the 1950's, the time of the "Cold War" nuclear scare and 'Sputnik.' For those of us who lived through it, we'll never forget the fear of the Russians and Communism. I was fortunate to live in America and to have my parents and family during this period of history.

Mom and Pop have five kids. I have a pretty older sister, two older brothers who tease me, then there's me and a younger kid brother. We moved from a small house to a large ranch house in the county when I was almost five.

Our house is one of the nicest in the area, as Pop's a builder. Mom's a housewife and mother. She always wears a yellow apron and spends lots of time in the kitchen and at her sewing machine in the breezeway. This is a neat room with windows that flip up. It has terrazzo floors and there's an ironing board, TV and Pop's wooden business desk.

Our house is decorated with blond furniture and floral wallpaper on one wall. There's a lot of gold leaf framed pictures of the Sacred Heart of Jesus and crucifixes hanging in the living room and hallway. During the season of Lent, there's always pieces of palm behind every crucifix, pieces that turn curly with little yellow threads.

Religious statues of the Blessed Virgin, St. Joseph, St. Anthony and other saints clutter our bedroom dressers. I don't have room for my comb and brush. Then, there's white candles in little blue glass holders which sit under the statues. Some of these statues have chips and are worn, but they always stand still on top of their lace doilies.

We pray to St. Anthony of Padua a lot. He is the patron saint of lost things. I'm sure he is in heaven and keeps busy by helping people find stuff. When Mom can't find the scissors, she always says a prayer to St. Anthony. Sometimes we all pray to St. Anthony as we search together, we run down the hallway saying, "St. Anthony help us!" We get so disappointed and mad if we still don't find the scissors. But sometimes St. Anthony just takes a little longer. The scissors always show up!

Mom especially loves St. Thérèse Lisieux, and mom has taught me to love this saint. Mom chose her name as my confirmation name. St. Thérèse's statue is very special. She's called "the Little Flower." She is very pretty and wears a brown nun's habit. She's got a crucifix and a bouquet of roses. There is a crack running down her back but she still looks pretty. She stands on my dresser in front of the mirror. I've got her prayer tucked into the corner of the mirror.

We've also got lots of rosaries, some with shiny crystal beads which are my favorite. They glisten like diamonds. Then there's some beads that glow in the dark. Mom's got the rosaries hanging on her dresser top like treasured necklaces. I don't like the scapulars, though. They're itchy and I once got hives from wearing one.

Bottles of holy water from Lourdes are in our home in case we get sick. One bottle sits near our rotary black telephone on a ledge in the hallway across from the doorbell. Did you know this water is not just holy water, but also comes from the grotto in Lourdes where Our Lady appeared? If you are sick, droplets of water can work a miracle! I think Mom has it by the telephone to remind her to use the Lourdes water first, before calling the doctor when we're sick.

In our new home, no one smokes, but there is always the smell of burning candles. We have an upstairs and a downstairs fireplace. The one upstairs is never used, but during the winter there is always a roaring fire down in the basement. Mom burns a variety of items in that fireplace. For some curious reason, our house looks different from the house of my Protestant friend next door.

Pop took me to my new Kindergarten class at the Parochial School; I am one of the youngest kids in the class. We have a lady teacher who is nice and dresses in normal clothes. The other teachers are called nuns and dress like St. Thérèse.

Before I entered school, I must say that some of my earliest memories were of guilt, even before my introduction to my Faith. As time progressed and I began to learn religion, prayer and sin seemed to be central in its emphasis and focus. Unbeknownst to me, the disorder was entering my mind, with its fierce edges attacking both emotions and reason. It was as if a steel key turned the lock on the door of this mental prison.

Chapter Three: Prayer at HOME

We had a sunny yellow tiled kitchen at home and Mom always prepared a nice dinner for the family, usually a hot meal along with a freshly baked pie. Pop would pair his meal with a small glass of red wine. The windows were always covered with steam from mom's cooking. It was comforting to be in the kitchen, what I thought, was my safety net. Together we said grace before meals and then we dug in. Praying as a group was not a problem; I had family to say when the praying was done. We chatted during the meal, usually about school or my brother's basketball game or my sister's new cashmere sweater.

After dinner, there's a 'thank you' prayer which we say by ourselves. I learned this prayer from the nuns. I'm on my last bite of food and I begin to worry about this prayer. I pick up my plate and don't help Mom with dishes. I hurry to my room and recite the prayer:

> *"We give Thee thanks for all Thy benefits, O Almighty God, who livest and reignest world without end. Amen. May the souls of the faithful departed, through the mercy of God, rest in peace. Amen."*

I repeat this prayer over and over. Did I say the words right? Did God hear my prayer? I'd better do it over. It is a sin to not say your daily prayers and after meal grace was a daily prayer! I could have just committed a sin!

It is now evening and I hear the melody of the ice cream truck coming down the street; traveling with its song "Pop Goes the Weasel" as it does every summer evening. I jump at this sound as it means the red and white truck is on its way! The highlight of my day is a grape snow cone; they are my favorite! I now hear the squeals of the neighbor children, Karen and Susan. I begin to get up, my mouth watering as I remember the taste of the snow cone I ate on Monday. But then I remember my task at hand. I stay rigid and continue to pray the after-dinner grace over and over. I decide I will give up my grape snow cone tonight as an offering for the souls in purgatory. After all, those souls are suffering terribly. I lift my head up briefly and see that the sun is now setting on the horizon.

An hour goes by and now it is time for nightly prayer. My siblings, Mom, and I kneel before the worn statue of the Blessed Mother, one which has years of accumulated candlewax. I pray the Rosary, only this time with the safety of Mom next to me. I take the Rosary, which glows in the dark, to bed with me.

Chapter Four: Parochial Grade School

At our parochial grade school, all the nuns were part of the same Catholic Order. The sisters lived in the same convent house which was small and attached to the schoolyard. The priests lived in a very large three-story brick home with tons of rooms. The Priests' home was right out in front and we were not allowed to step foot on that beloved lawn.

The sisters always wear a black habit with a veil that's got a big white piece of starched plastic above the brows. Nothing shows but their faces. Some are pretty and some are not; some have an acne problem, and some are old and have wrinkles. I wonder if they are blondes or brunettes? Sometimes the bushy eyebrows of the nuns, or those with a mustache, give it away. We never see their legs, so we can't see that hair.

The black habit has a long skirt, and they wear black socks and shoes. The black fabric is kind of shiny. Attached to the nuns' belts is a huge wooden rosary with a cross. When Sister Mary Rita walks down the hallway, we hear the knocking of the cross against the beads. The nuns do not wear any make up, not even lipstick. They are supposed to all be married to Jesus Christ. How could this be? You were only supposed to have one wife and they say Jesus was never married!

The sisters are always rushing and I think they're scared of the priests. Or maybe some like the priests? Sister Mary Edward is young and pretty. Every time she talks with the younger priest, she turns bright red!

The Sisters were pious and disciplined. They had chosen the convent as their vocation, and were ready to make that sacrifice. They were also trained to impose discipline upon the students. Their punitive stance assumed we all needed it. At times, loud scolding was heard and we knew the words echoed into the ego of the other small child. Humiliation was part of the accountability.

Catechism was the most important of the classes in which they taught. We knew the Baltimore Catechism in depth. Along with daily mass and prayers, we were well steeped in Catholicism as young children. There was a great deal of uniform ritualistic acts.

We have one teacher for each grade and we stay in the same classroom the whole long day. The teacher's an expert in all areas of arithmetic, penmanship, catechism, history and geography. She's gotta know it all. Funny thing, we never have a priest for a teacher. They just say mass, listen to confessions and go visit sick people. I wonder why the priests have things better than the nuns? Are they more blessed? Also, why are the Altar attendants always boys and not girls? We girls just sing in the choir. And when we grow up, why is it OK to join the convent and become a nun, but we can't be a priest? Well, mom already has my name picked out to be Sister Mary Rose, so I'd better just become a nun.

Our school uniform is a navy-blue dress and I wear white bobby socks and black and white saddles, with white shoelaces. The socks always gotta be turned over at the top. The yellow school bus picks me up very early in the morning, so we can go to Holy Mass before our classes. I'm always so tired in the morning, so Mom gives me a sponge bath on school mornings while I am still sleeping. After dressing, I gather my school books, my coat and mittens and I wait for the bus. I say my Morning prayers on the bus; I always sit in the same seat. How can I get my prayers done before the school bus gets here? I repeat my prayers over and over to be sure I say them right.

The bus driver's name is Pete and if it is a rainy morning he always says, "It's a good morning for ducks," as he uses the hand crank to open the heavy folded bus door. I got his autograph once. We make a few stops along the way picking up other students. The smell of gasoline on the bus makes me nauseous, especially when we have the windows open. In a short time, the yellow school bus arrives at school. We go to our classroom before walking into the Church. I'm not sure why we can't talk, but I spend this time praying. Sometimes I hum "Popeye the Sailor Man." My brother and I love this cartoon character! My favorite part is when Popeye eats the spinach and gets super strong.

One morning at the beginning of class, while reciting the Allegiance to the Flag, I must have slumped slightly while standing with the other students. The nun yelled, "Stand up straight and don't slump, Gina," and then said, "There you go, a nice girl!"

She used me as an example of poor quality in student posture. I was shocked and humiliated that she would scold me in front of the class. I didn't cry until I got home. Then the tears flowed.

We can't bring our lunch to school. The school cafeteria cooks lunch for us and charges Pop in the tuition. That's the way it works. As I enter the cafeteria, I become fearful as I see the nuns patrolling the lunchroom. My friends and I line up and take a green melamine tray from a stack. There are wrapped utensils, neatly folded for us. Volunteer moms dish out the food as we slide the trays down the metal slats. The Moms talk to each other, but never to us. I can already see the stewed tomatoes, smashed green peas and that stinky slice of meatloaf. Not again! Ah, but there is white bread and a carton of milk. We sit at the tables we're supposed to sit at. I say grace by myself. I'm hungry, but I don't like the looks of this food.

When we're finished, Sr. Mary Raphael gazes at us as and checks our tray before she scrapes any remnants into a large bowl. With her stern face, she judges if we've eaten enough. Last week, Bobby didn't like the stew and so she made him go back to the table to eat some more. After one bite, he gagged and vomited on the floor. I dreamed of saying, "Thank you very much Sr. Mary Raphael. Torture is a sin and save that one for Confession!" Dreams only. But, I've learned a trick, and that is to stuff a lot of food into the milk carton! I am always scared Sr. Mary Raphael will find out what I am doing! I check the milk carton repeatedly as I approach the nun.

There is a bright spot in the dreary lunch area: the candy counter in the back of the cafeteria. The candy bars are stacked evenly behind the gleaming glass and they look delicious. There are Hot Tamales packets, bags of M&M's with peanuts and packets of Atomic Fire Balls. I won't be hungry anymore if I get some candy.

I go out with the others into the Church parking lot for recess. I have lots of friends and during playtime, I forget about the praying and sinning. The other children attending the Parochial school don't have problems like mine. At least, I don't think so. But most are still afraid of the nuns and priests.

Chapter Five: Confession

Rollout the Sacrament of Penance, an established sacrament. It was a very special event in the Church by which our participation allowed us to receive God's forgiveness and grace. At our parochial school, we learned a lot about the Sacrament of Penance otherwise known as Confession.

One of the stipulations was, for the act of contrition to be complete, one must fulfill all the obligations that follow from one's sins. They said that if you stole something you must return what was stolen and be truly sorry. Confession was an **activity which** aggressively stirred the pot of OCD scrupulosity. The whole process was like a springboard for doubt and anxiety to soar. After my first confession, I was to go every Saturday in the afternoon to confess again.

It is a typical Saturday morning and I'm enjoying my crayons and coloring books, but I hurriedly push them aside. I have a job to do and that is to prepare for Confession this afternoon. Like last week, it is time to examine my conscience for any sins I may have committed. Thinking about all of the things I might have done wrong makes me sad, but it seems that I commit the same sins each week: I had been angry and fought with my brother, told a lie, etc. Even though they were the same sins as my last confession, I rehearse this set of sins at least 10 to 15 times. I am afraid that I will forget one. What if I die this week and God doesn't hear me repent for a sin because I forgot it?

And, besides, I need to have enough sins to make it appear I've done a good job preparing for the Holy Sacrament of Confession. I relive minute by minute of my week, examining each action I made with a fine-tooth comb.

Arriving at Church this afternoon, we make the sign of the cross with the holy water residing in the little reservoirs. This water is not the same thing as Lourdes water, but it is still holy enough. I am careful to not get it all over the terrazzo floor.

My brothers, sister and I wait in line to the side of the confessional booths. There are two booths on each side of the central aisle. They each have a door in the center and the side sections have purple velour curtains. Behind the center doors, there is a priest sitting comfortably and endowed with the authority to forgive our sins. But the priest is also bound by a law of secrecy. He can't tell anybody our sins, not even a police officer!

There is a long line on each side. Many sinners of all ages, children, mothers, fathers and old folks wait to get their souls cleansed. Waiting in this line is a penance in and of itself; everyone has a face with a sad and sorrowful expression. I am so afraid of this act, that many times I almost wet my pants.

The guy before me comes out of the confessional. He looks like his soul is cleansed! It is my turn next. Once behind the purple velour curtain, I kneel on the pew. I feel a lump in my throat and I can't swallow. My trembling is making the old pew quiver and I can feel the fissures in the broken plastic under my knees. I wait in silence and sorrow as the priest finishes the Confession of the person on the other side. I hear the other lattice door creak as the priest closes it and I know it is now my turn.

I carefully examine the pattern of the lattice door, and soon light begins to shine through the holes. The light was a flicker, but I could feel the strong voice.

I speak first, "In the Name of the Father, and of the Son, and of the Holy Spirit, Amen. Bless me Father for I have sinned. It has been one week since my last confession. These are my sins."

I rattle off my memorized sins of anger and lies, but this week I have a new sin, one which has caused me much anxiety.

"Also, Father, I stole two plastic price tags at the butcher counter at the A&P grocery store. They popped right out and I took them home."

I ask the priest, "Can I give the butcher 50 cents in exchange for the tags?"

The priest says, "No, just don't do it again."

I kept saying "Are you sure, are you sure Father?"

The priest remarks, "For your penance say five Hail Mary's. I absolve you of your sins in the name of the Father, and of the Son, and of the Holy Spirit. My child, please say your act of contrition."

A priest is the only one who can give us absolution besides God himself.

I say, "O my God, I am heartily sorry for having offended Thee, and I detest all my sins, because I dread the loss of Heaven and the pains of Hell, but most of all because they offend Thee, my God, who art all-good and deserving of all my love. I firmly resolve, with the help of Thy grace to confess my sins, to do my penance and to amend my life. Amen."

The priest then tells me to go in peace and he blesses me. My legs shaking, I stand up, and with a big sigh, I leave the ominous confines of the confessional.

Outside of the confessional, I move to a pew and begin my penance. I occasionally peak up to look at the line. It slowly dwindles until it is completely empty, and the emptiness of the church brings slight comfort. Maybe God can hear me better if I am alone. A few short minutes later, the door to the confessional creaks open and the priest appears. He gives me a slight nod and slowly shuffles to the front doors of the church. Once I hear the loud slam of the heavy front doors, I return to my prayers. I ask God for forgiveness for the interruption and I begin to continue. Then the doubt enters my mind. What if I'm not truly sorry for my sins? If not, my sins are not really forgiven. I repeat the prayer over and over. Fifty Hail Mary's later, I stand up exhausted and walk to the front doors. I stop and briefly examine the beautiful stained glass on the doors. The bright colors of red, green and yellow remind me of my crayons.

I snap out of my trance and push open the heavy mahogany church doors. Mom is sitting at the bottom of the church stairs patiently. She turns around and beams when she sees me walk out. I run down the stairs, grab her hand and we begin walking home. I am starting to feel relief as we trek our way through the town and get closer to home, but then I see the A&P store, the shiny butcher counter shimmering in the top left corner of the window.

I can feel my heart begin to flutter. A thousand thoughts are racing through my mind. Am I truly sorry for stealing the tags? Does God forgive me? Is this sin still on my soul? I feel a single tear begin to swell in my right eye as the weight of guilt swells up in my chest. I try as hard as I can to keep the tear from falling, but there was no hope. I feel the warm drop slowly travel down my face. The tear takes a brief pause on the bottom of my chin; it then falls off my chin and becomes like a dewdrop on the ground.

The next day Communion was agony. I was still in doubt about any new sins committed since yesterday's confession. It is sacrilege to receive Jesus with a mortal sin on your soul! But I don't think I committed any mortal sins since last night. At least I hope not.

Chapter Six: First Holy Communion

First Holy Communion was a big occasion for us Catholic families. The day of First Communion is one filled with family and friends. It was a very sacred event and only occurred after we had received the Sacrament of Penance with our first Confession. There was a lot of practice getting prepared for the big day. During our training, we learned that the Holy Communion hosts are consecrated unleavened hosts. They are made of wheat flour and water and the host is flat in shape and the size of a quarter. They become the body of Christ during Holy Mass, at the Consecration. We would receive the body of Christ on our tongue and we must try not to have the host touch our teeth.

On a bright sunny day in May, I recall Mom dressing me in a white full satin dress and a white net communion veil. I carried a special white prayer book and a Holy communion rosary. The rosary had white glass beads with a gold cross. White socks and black patent leather shoes adorned my feet. The spilling of light shined on my face climbing the Church steps. I felt very special and I remember the whole family came to Church for my First Communion. My family took up a whole pew and were ready to applaud as I walked down the aisle!

Looking like little brides with our white dresses and veils, we reverently marched down the aisle of the Church. The boys were equally as striking, being dressed in little suits. There was sacred music being played. We all looked so pious. In a celebratory fashion, white roses and carnations were plentiful. Tall gold candlesticks lined the aisles adorned with white candles with orange flickering flames. Ribbons of yellow and green light glowed through the patterns and pictures of the stain glass windows.

As the Holy Mass progressed and it was time to receive Our Lord, we formed a single line and approached the communion railing. The rail had cushioned pads for us to kneel on and served as a sort of grate to separate the altar area from the congregation. We kneeled at the communion railing, side by side, with hands folded perfectly together and upright. From a distance, the perfect row of girls with white dresses and veils sparkled like a garden of blossoming lilies.

The priest starts on one side of the rail and from the grand gold chalice, he lifts the Host and reverently gives it to each child. When it is my turn, I stick my tongue way out and hope the host does not drop. I'm lucky and take the Body of Christ without a problem. We each get up and follow behind the person in front, back to our pew. We kneel in the pew and piously bow our head in prayer for 2-3 minutes. We thank Jesus for coming into our hearts. I sure hope I thank Jesus enough. I still have my eyes closed in prayer long after the others have finished.

My family and I go home after the service to celebrate this sacred day. The aroma of Mom's homemade lasagna and stewed chicken fills the home. We have a feast in the dining room, our plates filled to the brim. I am about to finish my last bite of lasagna when I notice something. The Sacred Heart of Jesus picture has been gazing down at us this whole time. I slowly put down my fork and wonder: Had I just received the baby Jesus, or the Sacred Heart in Holy Communion? Which Jesus was it? Does it matter?

Chapter Seven: Lent and Easter

Traditionally, colorful eggs, coconut candy and chocolate bunnies are the joys of Easter for children. Mom would hand sew my outfit, my spring coat and always had a pair of cotton gloves for Easter Sunday. The coat was usually a pastel color of yellow or lavender, colors that sort of matched the Easter Eggs. Mom would purchase a couple of tiny baby Chickees that were covered in yellow fuzz and had orange beaks. Mom kept them in a cage in the kitchen and covered it with a towel. I looked forward to these each year. My siblings and I loved to pet them.

But, prior to the Easter Holiday, there was this huge mountain ahead of me called *Lent*. This was a difficult climb and not to be taken lightly. Historically, Lent is the time each year which represents the 40 days that Jesus wandered the desert praying and fasting after He was baptized.

At the beginning of Lent, there's Ash Wednesday, where we all got ashes on our foreheads. I try to keep this black smear visible and won't wash my face until morning. Then, there's fasting and penance leading to Holy Thursday, Good Friday, Holy Saturday and then Easter Sunday. I always "give up" candy for my penance during lent. It is hard though because Easter candy is everywhere. The sight of jelly beans, chocolate bunnies and marbled malt balls make my mouth water. I refuse to touch a piece, though.

During Lent, we aren't allowed to eat meat on Friday, and that includes the use of gravy and meat-based additives. I constantly check and recheck the container of sauce for evidence of chicken or beef broth before Mom uses it. I have to be sure! I am afraid to use butter on our fish because it is made of milk, which comes from a cow. I will do whatever it takes to avoid eating meat. After all, it's a mortal sin. I instead squeeze a bunch of lemon wedges on my fish. Better safe than sorry.

During Holy week, we perform the "Stations of the Cross" which demands absolute reverence. There are 14 ceramic painted plaques throughout the church, seven of which flank each of the two side walls of the Church. The pictures show the agony of the death of Christ. My brothers and I visit each station, dwell upon its meaning and whisper pleading prayers for forgiveness. My interpretation of the 14 plaques is the story of the crucifixion from the time Pilate said Jesus must die to the long and tragic carrying of the cross, the people who helped him, his death and removal from the cross. The station where Jesus fell is so terrible. Blood is everywhere. And the whole time he had that crown of pointy thorns that punctured his head. I'm glad that Simone guy stopped to help Jesus. I'm sure if my brothers were there, they would have done the same. I look at the plaques and try to feel the nails of Jesus in my hands. I begin to imagine what Jesus was feeling during this, the pain, the betrayal and the sorrow. His suffering was surely my fault due to my sinning! Can I ever be forgiven for causing His suffering? My knees are getting sore in the pews as I continue to worry. At least tomorrow we'll be one day closer to Easter and Jesus will be rising on Easter Sunday!

On Holy Saturday, my brother and I start dyeing Easter Eggs. We write our names in crayons before we dip them. Mom has a bunch of chipped and unmatched ceramic cups filled with vinegar and different colored dyes. I place my eggs in the pink and yellow dye. My kid brother puts his in the blue and green dye. We then place the colored eggs on green Easter grass on an oval plate. Mom already started pouring the yellow cake mix into the cast iron lamb mold. When the cake is done and cool enough, she decorates the lamb in coconut icing and makes a face with a cherry and chocolate chips. Mom then puts him on a plate with a pedestal. Our lamb represents The Lamb of Christ.

When I wake up later that night, I check the alarm clock. Is it after midnight yet? If so, I have one chocolate egg hidden under my pillow, and my Lenten fasting would be over. Yes, it is 1:00 am. I indulge. The chocolate tastes delicious. I return to my peaceful slumber. My brother and I find our

Easter baskets in the morning. The Easter Bunny always hides them.

Mom cook a lovely dinner for Easter. We always have a baked ham with pineapples slices and red cherries, deviled eggs, homemade ravioli and potato salad. Our Lambie cake is served for dessert.

In the meantime, the live chickees are in their cage. They will soon grow to become big chickens and run around our backyard! We always have chicken poop on the back-porch stairs. The neighbors thought they were pecking little pests, because they run into their yards. I never saw Pop end their lives so that mom could make fried chicken, but I know he did. Not to worry, mom will buy more chickees next Easter.

Chapter Eight: Guardian Angel

The concept of Guardian Angels, those angels appointed by God to protect and guide earthly creatures, has survived many centuries in many different religions and could be considered an ancient tradition. In fact, it was in the 15th century that there was deemed to be a "Feast of the Guardian Angels" which was added to the official calendar of Catholic holidays. To this day this devotion is held on October 2nd. Back in the fifties, we Catholics especially had an absolute reverence and belief in our Guardian Angel.

When I look at photos of Guardian Angels, I see huge, white airy looking wings with soft feathers. I think mine is a girl angel who has a pastel pink robe on and has long golden hair. Her large white wings flap quietly while she provides me safety and helps me to make good choices. She will stay with me for my whole life! I thank God for giving her to me. I say my prayer overnight to my guardian angel:

Angel of God
My guardian dear
To Whom His love
Commits me here
Ever this day
Be at my side
To light and guard
To rule and guide.
Amen.
*www.ewtn.com/Devotionals/prayers/angel2.htm

I wish I could see my Angel, but I know she is there and follows me everywhere. I can sometimes picture each student in my class sitting at their desks with their angel above or beside them. I'm glad when the classroom windows are open, so that the angels can flap their wings easier.

One morning after a good slumber, I woke up to find a white feather on the floor next to my bed. My first thought was that my guardian angel lost a feather during the night! It was surely a sign from God. I carefully placed that feather in a box where it resided for many years. At the time, I did not think of the feather filled pillow that I slept on, or the fact that our Tom cat loved to attack and eat birds in the yard! Both good reasons for a feather to be on the floor! It was better that I didn't.

But rather, it was definitely a feather from my angel and this thought propelled me for a long time. When I was in the throes of my scrupulosity, I frequently felt the need to repeat the guardian angel prayer at night. I was always in bed ready to fall asleep and now believe it was like counting sheep, the last thing before sleep was this prayer to my Angel, repeatedly.

Now there was an incident when there was no other explanation, but my being protected by a Guardian Angel. I was still a young child when Mom and I decided to go shopping one evening; we needed to take the bus. The bus stop was on the street which crossed ours. We were walking on the two-lane street near the soon to be Super Highway 70. We always caught the bus at this spot. I remember it was raining heavy that evening, so we both had an umbrella.

      Mom and I crossed the street and began walking north toward the construction. The sides of the road were muddy due to the construction and the heavy rain. I was walking behind Mom, holding on to her as my feet dug into the mud. I was sinking deeper and deeper. At one point, I had a fear that I was sinking into the mud, sort of a "quicksand" fear! I instinctively jumped to my right to protect myself. In doing so I had hopped directly on to the lane of the street with a car driving head on in the lane.

I fall onto the pavement and see in the distance an automobile's shining lights coming toward me. Terror strikes my heart and I hear Mom screaming, "Oh God, no!"

The next thing I see is the car screeching to a halting stop. I see the glaring lights and can feel the bumper of the car touching my hair. I look up and see the shiny front grill of the automobile. Where am I? What happened? I'm terrified.

My mother screamed and got me off the lane, hugging me for a long time! I was an inch from being run over and killed! Upon arriving home, I approached my hidden treasure box. I opened it to find the white feather and held it closely to my heart. Mom told the whole family how blessed we were to still have Gina!

Chapter Nine: Physical Manifestations

There were physical manifestations that accompanied my disorder. In the sixth grade, I weighed 64 pounds. I had to fight to keep weight on.

Why is it so hard to breathe? My heart is beating fast and I am inhaling deeply but I still cannot catch my breath. Over and over I have felt this sense of discomfort. I am breathing through my mouth a lot; I feel dizzy and my heart is beating fast. I tap my fingers on the railing of the stairs on the porch and I feel tingling. Over and over again I keep trying to catch my breath. Maybe I caught asthma from my brother? I remember yesterday at school this happened and now at home.

I did not realize that the abnormal breathing was a symptom of something deeper. Today I realize it was hyperventilation in a child! The anxiety from my disorder provoked hyperventilation, adding to the labyrinth of my suffering.

One of the baffling aspects of the illness was the degree of variation of the symptoms. There were times I felt normal, then the symptoms would, without warning, take possession. Mercurial, symptoms rising and falling as they pleased.

It's a beautiful spring day, and we arrive at Northland shopping center by way of the bus. My favorite place is Woolworths five and dime on the far corner. We buy some various kitchen items and then we stop at the luncheon counter. There are red swivel chairs on chrome bases around the shiny counters. I pick up the laminate menu even though I already know what I want. My favorite food here is the BLT sandwich on toast. I like how they cut the sandwich into little crunchy triangles, standing them up with toothpicks around a mound of French fries.   We each have a nice piece of pie for our dessert. The pie pieces sit on white

china plates as they nestle inside the little rotating plastic fixture. People can pick and choose their favorite flavor!

After lunch, we go over to Famous Barr for Mom to shop in the material department. Mom shops here frequently as she loves to sew. We begin looking at checkered material when out of nowhere, I start to shake and feel dizzy; I am trembling and scared. Terror overcomes me without a reason and I feel it a while before I say anything. Mom bends down to listen and she quickly carries me out of Famous-Barr.

It is chilly and windy outside. I fall behind my mother on the ground crying, with my hands on my eyes and ears. I remember a lady mannequin with a yellow spring hat being in the window of where I fell. "Mom, oh Mom I am so scared. I think I am going to die!" Mom covers me with her coat and hugs me until I stopped crying. She is also scared and embarrassed. Mom flags down a taxi to bring us home. The taxi driver wonders and exclaims, "Ma'am what did you do to your child? Is she a bad girl? Well, kids need a good whoopin' every now and then." Mom just shook her head.

We're now safely at home and Mom opens our medicine cabinet. What can she give me? There's just iodine and aspirin. Mom decides to give me an aspirin. Exhausted, I fall asleep.

In reflecting, Mom was hoping none of her acquaintances had witnessed the event at the shopping center. How would she explain it to a friend? "My daughter is crazy?" Mom did not understand the significance of panic attack in a child. She would avoid the subject due to shame and stigma of a possible mental illness!

Later in the month, at the same shopping center at Northland there was a contest-A Hula-Hoop contest! These were all the fad and we kids loved to practice in the yard. I signed up for the competition. My hoop was of aluminum as opposed to bright colored plastic hoops, as the others had. Thousands of children were spread out on the spacious Northland shopping mall parking lot. We twirled and spun those hoops to loud music and a lot of yelling fans! The momentum and excitement was mounting.

Getting close to the end, I pushed harder. I needed to prove that I was the best! My anxiety jump-started my breathing problem, and I found it harder to keep my hoop up. I thought a heart attack was pending. I prayed that God would help me! But with the pressure to breathe I could not concentrate on the twirling; I dropped the hula-hoop with a clatter and I was eliminated. I still could not catch my breath and began crying. It was such a disappointment and Pop would not be proud of me, as I am a loser. Why did God not hear my prayer? I became angry and now I had another sin on my soul!

Chapter Ten: Sexuality

While on a camping trip with a social group, I was introduced to the concept of sex. We had the usual campfire and marshmallows. Afterword, my girlfriend asked to join me in my sleeping bag to snuggle. As girlfriends do, we chatted a long time before we thought about closing our eyes. She then told me something shocking, and since my friend was older than me by two years, I did not question the validity of her remarks.

She said, "Did you know there is an opening down in your private parts other than one in your butt? That's where a man puts his penis in and that's what makes babies. It feels really good and married couples do it a lot."

I was baffled with the idea and couldn't comprehend.

I remarked, "Certainly that is not how my parents made babies!"

She reiterated, "That is the only way babies are made."

Confusion and guilt about this discussion were forming a strong web in my scrupulous OCD mind. Instead of being educated by a parent or teacher of the miracle of sex and birth, I found out through a girlfriend in a sleeping bag. I also thought I had committed a sin in discussing sex, as my first impression was this sounded nasty. Impure thoughts? Now a smothering guilt prevailed and I proceeded to Confession to plead for forgiveness. "Father forgive me for the impure thoughts I had." The priest gave me the routine penance.

There was also an incident at school which provoked anxiety and stirred my OCD before I was in puberty. Here is what happened:

While in class, restroom breaks are twice per day. Even if I have to go pee in between, I hold it, as I am scared to raise my hand. At exactly a quarter to 10:00 a.m. and a quarter to 2:00 p.m., we get up from our little wooden desks. A single line forms and we walk down the hall in unison to the girls' lavatory. Quiet is a must. The lavatory has speckled terrazzo floors with green walls and sinks with earthy smelling Lava soap. We take turns as we enter the creaky stalls.

It was one Thursday in May, that it happened, this strange experience. There was in full sight an unwrapped very used sanitary napkin sitting above the toilet, a shocking sight in a private school.

Another girl saw it and shrieked "Oh, how horrible!"

It was reported to the Principal. The norm would have been to call maintenance to clean it up and be done with it. Instead the nuns made it into a huge event.

All of us girls were called into a meeting.

The nun asked, "I want all of you who use sanitary pads to stand on one side of the room and those who do not, stay on this side."

I was almost eleven and blossoming but not yet in menstruation, so I remained; most of the other girls went to the other side. I was so very humiliated as the other girls stared. Sadly, the teacher thought this distinction would provide her a better audience. The other girls were scolded in the event the pad was left by one of them.

For me, it led to intimidation and humiliation. I now felt that I was different and my lack of puberty became an obsession from that point on; I was constantly checking my underpants for a spot of blood. I needed to feel adequate and like the other girls. My OCD again attacked my adolescent mind.

As I matured and did begin menstruation, Mom gave me a book and some sanitary napkins. There was no "let's talk about this now" moment; I was expected to read the book and understand. I was proud that I was now like the other girls! As far as sanitary disposal at home, Mom had a strict rule; she needed to burn the used pads in the downstairs fireplace. Why? Was it an attempt to get rid of what was natural? Or the fear that Pop or my brothers could see the pad in the trash? All I knew is that I had a collection of wrapped used sanitary napkins on the first shelf of my bedroom closet, waiting for the next fire in the basement fireplace!

Chapter Eleven: Purgatory and Indulgences

During the month of August, it was still summer vacation and it was hot outside with mosquitoes buzzing. There was no air conditioning yet, and Mom had fans only in a few rooms in the house. I loved the outdoors and played in the woods with my friends during those summer days. We had a favorite spot by a gurgling brook that had a large white rock. We used to visualize an Indian man and woman having met on the white rock and falling in love. We therefore called it "Lovers' Rock." On sunny days, we'd walk into the woods and do what kids do. We'd watch the ripples of water circling the "Lovers' Rock" with such a sense of peace.

Small yellow flowers grew wild. During these times, I was happy.

But my OCD Scrupulosity took no vacation during the summer. The month of August was also devoted to the Immaculate Heart of Mary. I did a lot of reading in Mom's blue prayer book in the afternoons, the one with the gold leaf pages and blue leather binding. The name of the book is simply "The Prayer Book."

On page 73, there was a listed section: <u>August The Immaculate Heart</u>, referring to the heart of Mary. It includes prayers with the reward of indulgences. In the middle of the page is listed INVOCATIONS:

> **"O heart most pure of the Blessed Virgin Mary, obtain for me from Jesus, a pure and humble heart." ***
>
> *Indulgence of 300 days to say once, plenary indulgence once a month on the usual conditions for the daily*

> *devout repetition of this invocation. (387)*

"Sweet heart of Mary, be my salvation." *

Indulgence of 300 days; plenary indulgence once a month on the usual conditions, if repeated daily. (386)

On page 323 of same the Prayer Book, it explains:

> *Many of the prayers in this book carry indulgences granted by the Church. This fact is always noted immediately after a particular prayer. The number in the parentheses following each indulgence corresponds to the number given to each prayer in the <u>Enchiridion Indulgentiarum</u>, the latest edition of the Church's official manual of indulgenced prayers and devotions.**

Now we were taught that being in Purgatory was temporary; it is for the Souls of the dead who die with some punishment still coming, due to their sins. Like if you die between confessions and you've sinned. These souls raise up to purgatory for suffering and purifying before going to heaven. We don't know how long we may be there. Indulgences earned would take away from the time you were doomed to spend in Purgatory.

After reading about this, my heart soared with hope as this was a way for me to keep my soul from suffering. I wrote this prayer down very carefully.

I repeat this invocation over and over and hope that I'm being devout enough? "O heart most pure of the Blessed Virgin Mary, obtain for me from Jesus, a pure and humble heart. Sweet heart of Mary, be my salvation." I make sure there is no noise in

the room, that I'm on my knees and hands folded upright. Dwelling on the imagined fire and doomed suffering of my soul in Purgatory, my heart is now thudding and my pulse is pounding. I must build up days, years or hit the biggest, a plenary indulgence. I am fatigued and exhausted from the puzzle of different prayers and days of redemption. Dear God, am I being devout enough?

I must continue; it is hard to swallow and my mouth is dry. To keep track of my time built up, I design a Journal for Purgatory. With my crayons, I enter the amount of days I earned, which prayer I said and which date I said it. With different colored crayons, red, green and yellow, I separate these into columns. I continue to add the days in my Purgatory Journal.

I'm up to 3400 Indulgence days now! But, anxiety stuck its ugly head again with the thought: How am I going to get this journal to God to show Him? What if I added wrong? What if I lose the journal when I grow up? And which sins are equal to a Purgatory day? Am I confused about the whole thing? Is my sin of fighting with Michael equal to a hundred days in purgatory? Or 300 days? I am now lost in a kaleidoscope of Purgatory plans. My crayons are worn and the Scrupulosity is magnifying and festering. I must hide this precious Purgatory Journal and buy new crayons.

*The Prayer Book, Beautiful and helpful prayers from ancient and modern sources, The Catholic Press, Inc. Copyright 1954, Imprimatur, Samuel Cardinal Stritch Archbishop of Chicago

SECTION 3

Chapter Twelve: When I told Mom

I cannot remember exactly when I told Mom of my suffering, or which experience prompted me to do so. The mental disorder had beaten me badly. All I knew was that I needed HELP! I could not do this alone anymore. Lying in bed one Sunday afternoon, I just let it out:

I said, "Mom there is something wrong with me and I don't know what to do."

She asked, "What do you mean?"

I told her, "I keep saying my prayers over and over again. I cannot stop. I am worried all of the time about going to Confession."

She replied, "Maybe you are becoming scrupulous, Gina?"

I then immediately said, "Mom, is being scrupulous a mortal or a venial sin?"

The disorder had now stained my childhood ability to reason.

I began to tremble and to cry. Mom held me tightly and told me that I had not committed a sin at all and I should not worry so much. She realized that I needed help, so she called our family doctor. She kept me home from school the next day. I can remember shivering, as if I was cold. Mom stayed close to me and I could see her eyes darkening with sadness. Her quivering lower lip was obvious as she talked to her friend. She held back her tears as if in doing so, she was protecting me. She stayed and held me closely until I fell asleep each night. Pop did not begin to understand this illness. My nose was not running and I didn't have a stomach ache. Why was I in bed?

When we visited the doctor, Mom was timid and had a few words with him during which she explained my worrying. I do not believe Mom brought up the ideation of sin and prayer to the doctor. I think she simply indicated that I was pale, thin and worried too much.

The Doctor sat me down and said to me, "Gina, why do you carry the world on your shoulders little girl?"

He examined my blood pressure and checked my throat etc. He did not find any physical symptoms other than my being very thin. He told mom to keep me rested and to watch for any further symptoms.

We got into the cab and went home; no progress having been made. When I was resting in my bed, Mom brought in the precious bottle of Lourdes water.

She asked, "Gina can I sprinkle this Lourdes water on you?"

I thought, "Why not?"

Mom sprinkled the Lourdes holy water on me repeatedly. My pajamas were soaked but I felt blessed. We prayed that Our lady of Lourdes would heal me.

Mom continued to be close to me during those several weeks at home. We waited for the Lourdes water to start working. She held me closely and prayed her Rosary. Her friends sent prayers also. Mom mostly told them I was fatigued and needed rest. I slept a lot and felt the most relaxed when there was no stimulation. For some reason, I did not want my little brother in the room. Somehow, my sweet little brother, my best friend, seemed to soar my anxiety.

How did Mom handle it with the school? There were no conference or phone calls with the school or teacher to discuss my illness or alternative options. Mom was frightened of the situation, *but more frightened of the nuns and priest.*

Although no drugs or real therapy was given, after a month or so, I was now able to motivate and remembered to rest when I became anxious. Mom allowed less frequent Confession and prayers and encouraged more free time in the evenings. But, because we had not identified the illness, I still did not know how to shut it off. The more I rested and the more protected I felt, and the less the OCD Scrupulosity raged. But I was anxious to get back to my studies and to see my friends in school.

For absenteeism at our Parochial school, protocol was for the parent to write a note upon return to class. Mom practiced the note as she finally wrote, *"Please excuse Gina's absence as she had nervous problems,"* and that was the extent of the communication with the school. I was returned to the same class at the same school with the same scolding nun! I told my friends I had issues with my "nerves." They did not think too much of it, which was a relief.

●○■□■○●

Chapter Thirteen: Recovery

In retrospect, I believe the scrupulosity aspect of the OCD diminished slowly with rest and change. I had to relax more. I did not try to rationalize anything; I was too young for that. Instead, I thought of things which brought happiness. I did deep belly breathing which the doctor told me to do. These were simple techniques but were acquired only with time. But I must make a distinction: the eventual healing from scrupulosity was not like any other curative process. There was not a time when a light went off and I thought, "I'm finally feeling better now, I'm not counting and doubting so much!" Or when I sighed and thought, "Oh I am so glad that feeling of fear is gone and behind me!" My mind did not process, nor recognize the progress of healing.

As a person, I am blessed with resilience. I still had memories, but they were less frequent and new positive thoughts prevailed. Although the feature of scrupulosity subsided, there were residual symptoms, but they were manageable. However, my anxiety was a part of me and remained.

As I entered the next grade, a new teacher arrived and was assigned to our class. The new sister was like a breath of sunshine in my life. She herself was timid, reserved and most of all, kind. She did not scold students but carefully gave constructive criticism. She encouraged each of us to have our own individuality. With less focus on punishment on more on love of people and of God, I began to heal. I've learned that God does send angels into our lives, and she was one of them.

My confessions were less frequent and I began to enjoy Mass as I was now singing in the choir. We received accolades for our performance. I began singing my heart out.

I began to enjoy life and to build good memories. One of which is Christmas memory from that very year.

It was Christmas Eve and sleet hit our picture window pane with a sound like shattering glass. The wind made the temperature more gripping than ever, making howling sounds. Our Christmas tree was a live fir balsam which sat in a bucket of sand, the sand being from Pop's garage. The tree had big, orange, blue, red green and yellow shining lights. We hung atomic ornaments and silver tinsel. The nativity set at the bottom was very visible and had a single illuminating white light. The story of the birth of Jesus was wonderful; I enjoyed dwelling on the shepherds and the three kings. The Christmas tree sat directly in front of the picture window and was glowing.

We sat as a family enjoying cocoa and Christmas cookies. In the distance, we saw the silhouettes of a small group of brave Christmas Carolers who were singing "Silent Night" while approaching our home. It was a beautiful sight. We greeted them through the front door and gave a donation. Moments of joy such as these were coming into my life and I could feel them without anxiety and doubt.

Continuing my story into later years, we studied mental health during my health class in High School. There was a segment on OCD. It was like bingo; a light went on in my head! A blaring discovery. That is what I had as a child! You mean other people had this same thing? The recognition that it was an established mental disorder scared me, but also gave closure to the mystery. That realization was an Epiphany to my life! But I still did not tell Mom.

With the passing of time, I was treated correctly with psychotherapy and antidepressants, which controlled the anxiety and OCD. As an adult, I am high functioning, having climbed the ladder in my professional career. I continue taking medication.

A smaller Epiphany happened later in life, when I discovered some relevant information about St. Thérèse of Lisieux. While growing up, Mom encouraged me to have so much devotion to this saint. I truly loved St. Thérèse; my final prayer every night was to her. I've discovered that St. Thérèse of Lisieux is quite ironically the patron saint for OCD! Historically, before she became a nun, St. Thérèse also suffered from the disorder. Here is a quote:

> Thérèse also suffered from scruples, a condition experienced by other saints such as Alphonsus Liguori, also a Doctor of the

Church and Ignatius Loyola, the founder of the Jesuits. She wrote: 'One would have to pass through this martyrdom to understand it well, and for me to express what I experienced for a year and a half would be impossible.' *

*Monahan, Joan. Therese of Lisieux, 2003, ISBN 0-8091-6710-7, p. 45

Mom knew nothing about Obsessive Compulsive Disorder, yet she taught me to reach out to St. Thérèse. Coincidence or divine intervention? ***You can be the judge.***

SECTION FOUR

Conclusion:

After reading the sections of my memoir, can we flash forward to the year 2018?

From my memoir, I hope you've

captured the sense of a mental disorder that is an extreme aberration for the victim. A disorder with a need for it to be approached and monitored with great care, by both parents and educators.

We can see that in modern times, the strict European cultural practices have faded and evolved into a more open and healthy relationship between parents and children. With the change in generations, those children who are now parents have raised their children with different approaches in social interaction and in practices of Faith. Would you agree that this is a very positive step forward?

Currently, I understand there are progressive treatments available for OCD; I've read about certain SSRI drugs, in addition to Cognitive Behavior Therapy, specifically one type entitled *Exposure and Respond Prevention*. Professionals in the field can assess the appropriate treatment for a child;

teams of Psychoanalysts and Psychiatrists, whether in private or clinical practice, are available to help.

A note of emphasis; I must shout to parents out there, embrace these opportunities **and go for help if you suspect abnormal obsessive or compulsive behavior**! Most importantly, stay cognizant of your children's moods and state of mind, not only in religiosity, but in everyday behavior.

Epilogue:

What have I learned? Realizing that forgiveness and acceptance is a foundation for healing, that it lays the groundwork. I have accepted the disorder. I would not be me without having had it.

During adult psych treatment, I was treated for my perception of the unhealthy emotional treatment I endured. Gradually, I began to comprehend others' suffering and reasons for behavior. Also, by recognizing and dwelling on the love of God, *rather than imagined punishment*, acceptance began for me. By recognizing the value of past traditions and culture, I could see a positive side. I had developed a level of self-discipline that is immeasurable. My sense of spirituality has changed and grown over the years. Besides, didn't I get most of my purgatory out of the way? Well maybe, Vatican II made some adjustments to my purgatory, after all. There was a silver lining along with the dark clouds but it took me years to see it. I began treatment with SSRI medication and the biological road to recovery began.

In concluding, isn't change a constant in life? As we change, we grow. We need not fear change, but embrace it along with God's graces.

Spirituality: Calvary Cemetery

The deceased are held in great reverence by both the Church and immigrant culture, which is a sacred thing. These memories are not related to my OCD disorder in any way, but are beautiful recollections; experiences which contributed to my spirituality as it exists today.

Calvary Cemetery in St. Louis, MO was founded in 1857 and currently has over 300,000 graves and 470 acres of land. It is a Roman Catholic cemetery and owned by the Archdiocese of St. Louis. It is home to some of the original prairie grasses in the area. It is an enormous cemetery where many famous people are buried, Tennessee Williams, Dred Scott, Kate Chopin, to name a few. I should interject I will be buried there but I'm not famous. The location is on West Florissant near Highway 70. For me, this location has a special meaning. You see, I was born at the clinic on the north side, my wedding reception was across the street and the cemetery is on the opposite side. I was born, married and will be buried all on the same corner!

Entering the cemetery, beauty abounds from the beautiful trees and greenery, to the ornate tall archangel monuments and headstones. Many are of architectural interest. There are stone vestibule mausoleums with heavy doors with doorknockers, containing crypts. These were made to resemble homes. A variety of messages adorn the stones, but usually contain the birth and death date of the deceased.

I have vivid memories as a young child visiting there; my ancestors are all buried within those iron gates. Pop would bring us after Mass on Sunday to visit our loved ones, especially my maternal grandmother. It was a cultural act of reverence to visit and say prayers for the souls of the departed. Mom was especially devoted to that thought; being traditional, visiting the final resting place was also fulfilling a perceived sense of obligation.

Winding and twisting roads meander through the vast land of the cemetery. The stark gray sky matches the color of the stone tombstones. We always heard the soft ringing and rolling of the church bells, echoing across the empty and barren land giving us solace as we faced our own mortality.

On that December Sunday, Pop drove us to the section in which Grandma is buried. She passed away in 1943 and her grave site is deep into the interior of the section and can't be seen from the road.

Pop picks me up out of our Ford sedan and I follow Mom. My rubber boots are crunching in the snow, and the wind is howling. We trudge forward as I pull up the leggings of my snowsuit. I have earmuffs on and my

plastic-coated mittens. Mom always wears a dress with nylons so I am really worried about her legs getting cold under her coat.

Mom says, "I know it is cold, but all we have to do is look for that poor Polish boy's grave and we'll find Mom." You see, the stone of the 'polish boy' is large with his name engraved and a photo embossed. He is buried next to Grandma. Easy to spot. We trudge deeper, our feet getting numb from the snow, but we still cannot see it. Finally, straight ahead is the anticipated tombstone of the 'Polish boy' and there is Grandma buried directly to the right. We breathe a sigh of relief. Grandma's gray tombstone appears to be so barren. Mom places the brightly decorated Christmas wreath on grandma's grave; the vivid colors separate it from the others and make it distinct. We recite:

"Eternal rest, grant unto them, O Lord, and let perpetual light shine upon them. May

the souls of the faithful departed through the mercy of God rest in peace. Amen." ∗

∗Prayer Source: Catholic Family Handbook, The by Rev. George A. Kelly, Random House, Inc., New York, 1959

Mom always cries at her Mom's grave. The tears are almost freezing as they roll down her cheeks. I watch her as we pray in silence afterword. I am still repeating the Eternal Rest prayer, as I think I did not say it with enough devotion. She is remembering her Mom and how much she misses her in our lives. We sometimes say a prayer for the Polish boy, also. We then slowly return to Pop patiently waiting on the road.

In reflection, the grave of the 'Polish boy' was always embedded in my memory, as an adult I still look for it as a marker to find Grandma's spot. It wasn't until I was married, that I noticed my last name was the same name as the 'Polish boy's.' All those years staring at that gravestone! What a surprise, when I realized I had grown up to marry the 'Polish boy's' nephew! What are the chances he would be buried exactly next to my Grandmother all those years ago? Was it coincidence or destination?

In later years when I was in my late sixties, I continued to visit my loved ones in Calvary Cemetery. My husband, a grandchild of mine and my older brother had since joined my parents and my grandparents at Calvary. It is a very special place. On a windy gray day in the autumn, when the ground was covered with yellow and crimson leaves, my fiancé and I visited nine different grave sites within the many sections of Calvary.

The focus of the story involves a lost article in the huge cemetery. On that day, we both had key fobs to my modern automobile. Grandma's grave was the second site we visited, the grave still being very deep from the road. We were on the last and ninth site in an entirely different section, when I discovered something. Somewhere in the vastness of the cemetery with all the piles of leaves and ruts, I had dropped and lost my key fob. We had been driving on his fob for the past half hour! I knew to replicate the fob would be hundreds of dollars. We were both so upset! But I remembered something from my past.

I remarked, "Don't worry St. Anthony will find the key fob."

My fiancé although a religious man responded, "Oh really, Gina?"

We quickly drove the winding lanes and we retraced our steps. We searched diligently and found nothing at the first section. I prayed, "Please, St. Anthony, help us!" I also prayed to my Grandma. As we once again approached her grave, our shoes were sinking deeper into the mound of leaves. We walked in circles and we were getting so frustrated. We approached her grave from the side and there ahead about fifty feet from the street, sticking with only its yellow labeled top was the key fob! A flash from heaven, with the vastness of the land and the autumn covered ground, there was the lost treasure! My first thought was "it must be somebody else's! It can't be mine. It was so coincidental that I'd found it hard to believe.

We then went on our way, but not before thanking good old St. Anthony! He had worked a "mini miracle." Or could it have been my dear Grandma whom I had never met? Tears filled my eyes. Divine intervention? Or maybe all the above.

Changes with Vatican II:

A few comments on the Church in the 1950's and the changes which came with the Second Vatican Council:

From history, we know the fifties were a time in the Church when all the traditional rituals were still in place to include a Latin Mass, the form of the ancient Requiem "Mass for the Dead", feast days, octave and vigils of feast days to name a few. We used what I believe was called the "Marian Missal." Mine was leather and had gold etched pages, the paper of the pages was thin like onion skin. At the Mass, the priest faced the other way as the entire altar was against the wall; the additional table concept had not yet been introduced. In the pews we saw the back of the priest as he said Mass. Latin was the language of choice to be used in prayers and hymns. These traditions were all the norm.

Then, on Jan 25, 1959, Pope John XXIII announced the Second Vatican Council, 21st ecumenical council of the Roman Catholic Church to be held at a future date (1962–65). It opened on Oct. 11, 1962. This could be deemed as a real revolution for the Roman Catholic Church. The goal of this Council was to bring the Church into the contemporary world, and it was successful in many ways. Catholics were now allowed to pray with other Christian denominations, and the Council encouraged relationships with other non-Christian faiths. Plus, the option for other languages besides Latin was introduced for Holy Mass. Different approaches for education and divine revelation were presented.

A quote about indulgences after Vatican 2:

> To overcome the confusion Paul VI issued a revision of the handbook (*Enchiridion* is the formal name) of indulgences. Today, numbers of days are not associated with indulgences. They are either plenary or partial...Pope Paul VI declared, '[T]he Church invites all its children to think over and weigh up in their minds as well as they can how the use of indulgences benefits their lives and all Christian society... Supported by these truths, holy Mother Church again recommends the practice of indulgences to the faithful. It has been

very dear to Christian people for many centuries as well as in our own day. Experience proves this' (*Indulgentarium Doctrina*, 9 & 11). *

*https://www.catholic.com/tract/myths-about-indulgences

    These changes brought about during The Vatican II Council are all available in the Catholic archives. There are many chapters of reading. A special note to be made is that Pope John XXIII was later canonized as a Saint of the Church for his merits of opening the Vatican II Council. He was indeed a "spiritual hero."

    Have we not lived during a time of great change, one which continues to shower reflections of hope? I believe so. We now see that spirituality and love for God bring wisdom to the soul, embracing our beings as we go forward in life!

Printed in Great Britain
by Amazon